Mastering Public Speaking with Assertiveness Techniques

Table of Contents

1. Introduction 1

2. The Basics of Public Speaking 2

    2.1. The Essence of Public Speaking 2

    2.2. Breaking Down the Speech Process 2

    2.3. Preparing for Your Speech 3

    2.4. Delivering a Successful Speech 3

    2.5. Reflecting on Your Performance 4

    2.6. Overcoming Public Speaking Anxiety 4

3. Assertiveness 101: Understanding the Concept 6

    3.1. The Nature of Assertiveness 6

    3.2. Assertiveness vs Aggression 7

    3.3. Importance of Assertiveness in Public Speaking ... 7

    3.4. Achieving an Assertive Communication Style ... 8

    3.5. In a Nutshell 8

4. Building Confidence: Step into Your Power 10

    4.1. Understanding Confidence 10

    4.2. Importance of Self-Talk 10

    4.3. Emphasize Body Language 11

    4.4. Dress for Confidence 11

    4.5. Master Your Material 12

    4.6. Seek Constructive Feedback 12

    4.7. Embrace Failure 12

    4.8. Nurture Your Well-Being 13

5. The Power of Voice: Techniques for Effective Delivery ... 14

    5.1. Understanding Your Voice 14

    5.2. Fine-Tuning Your Voice 15

    5.3. Voice Modulation Techniques 16

    5.4. Practice Makes Perfect 16

6. Mastering Body Language: Silent yet Powerful Communication . . 18

6.1. Understanding the Basics of Body Language. 18

6.2. Reading Your Audience's Body Language. 19

6.3. Practicing and Modifying Your Body Language. 19

6.4. How to Use Body Language Effectively. 20

6.5. Enhancing Confidence: The Power Pose. 20

7. Crafting Impactful Speeches: The Art of Effective Preparation . . . 22

7.1. Know Your Audience 22

7.2. Structuring Your Speech 23

7.3. Introduction 23

7.4. Body 23

7.5. Conclusion 24

7.6. Practicing Out Loud 24

7.7. Prepare for the Unexpected 25

8. Using Assertiveness Techniques in Real-Time Scenarios 26

8.1. Understanding Assertiveness 26

8.2. The Pillars of Assertiveness 26

8.3. Assertiveness Techniques for Public Speaking 27

8.4. Assertiveness Skills in Real-Life Scenarios 28

9. Managing Anxiety and Nerves: Stay Calm & Confident 30

9.1. Understand Your Anxiety 30

9.2. Reframing Anxiety as Excitement 30

9.3. Preparing and Practicing Your Speech 31

9.4. Power Poses and Physical Relaxation Techniques 31

9.5. Visualize Your Success 32

9.6. Leverage Nervous Energy 32

10. Interacting with the Audience: Learn to Engage Effectively 33

10.1. Understand Your Audience 33

10.2. Understand Your Content 33

10.3. Establish a Connection 34

10.4. Encourage Interaction 34

10.5. Look and Listen 34

10.6. Use Visual Aids 35

10.7. Overcome Challenges 35

11. Continuous Improvement: Tools and Techniques for Ongoing Growth 36

11.1. Honing a Growth Mindset 36

11.2. Embracing the Power of Reflection 37

11.3. Implementing Feedback Loops 37

11.4. The Art of Incremental Changes 38

11.5. Constant Practice and Exposure 38

11.6. Learning from Others 38

11.7. Conclusion 39

Chapter 1. Introduction

Unlock your potential as a dynamic communicator with our Special Report, "Mastering Public Speaking with Assertiveness Techniques." Speaking in public may sound daunting, but the magic unfolds once you master the art of making speeches, conversation, or presentations with confidence. This report is designed to be your empowering guide, packed with useful, easy-to-implement tools and techniques that allow you to not only get your point across effectively but also to command respect and attention. Whether you're gearing up for a career that requires regular public speeches or simply aspire to amplify your voice and refine your persuasion skills, this lighthearted yet deeply insightful report is just the ticket. Get ready to transform your public speaking skills and capture audiences like never before!

Chapter 2. The Basics of Public Speaking

Understanding the basics of public speaking is grounded in the fundamentals of communication. To master the art of delivering compelling messages in a public forum, we need to start with the bedrock principles that make a speaker effective and influential.

2.1. The Essence of Public Speaking

Public speaking isn't just about standing up and speaking to an audience; it's about engaging your listeners, conveying your ideas clearly, and stimulating an audience reaction. The essence of public speaking lies in understanding your audience and delivering your message in a way that resonates with them.

Remember, your role as a speaker isn't to just provide information; you're also required to guide the thinking of your listeners, motivate them to act, and lead them towards a decision or understanding.

2.2. Breaking Down the Speech Process

A successful public speech involves several stages: preparation, presentation, and post-performance analysis.

1. Preparation: This initial phase is when you reflect on your topic, your audience's interests, and how to deliver your message effectively. This stage involves extensive research, outlining your speech, and rehearsing it.

2. Presentation: This is the most visible part of the process, where you deliver your speech to your audience. Good presentation

involves effective body language, clarity of speech, use of visual aids, and audience engagement.

3. Post-Performance Analysis: This stage offers an opportunity to reflect on your performance, gather feedback, and identify areas for improvement.

All three stages are equally crucial in the speech process, and a nuanced understanding of each can greatly enhance your public speaking skills.

2.3. Preparing for Your Speech

Begin your preparation by understanding your audience and the purpose of your speech. Are you to inform, persuade, entertain, or inspire? Knowing your goal will help shape the content and structure of your speech. A well-researched, carefully planned speech not only resonates with your listeners but also boosts your confidence as a speaker.

Next, outline your speech to ensure a logical flow of ideas. Start with a compelling introduction that hooks the audience, followed by well-structured main points supported by evidence or examples, and close with a powerful conclusion that reinforces your main message.

Rehearsing your speech is also essential for a smooth delivery. It allows familiarization with the content, gives a feel of the timing, and aids in refining aspects such as tone, pace, and emphasis.

2.4. Delivering a Successful Speech

The main components of effective speech delivery include body language, voice modulation, and audience engagement.

1. Body Language: Effective body language can significantly enhance the impact of your speech. Maintain eye contact, use

hand gestures to emphasize points, and project confidence through your stance and movement.

2. Voice Modulation: Variation in your tone, pace, and emphasis can make your speech more engaging. Speak slowly and clearly, adding pauses for emphasis and allowing your audience time to absorb your message.

3. Audience Engagement: Interacting with your audience keeps them involved and responsive. Ask rhetorical questions, share personal experiences, and make your content relatable for the audience.

The key to a successful delivery is authenticity. Be yourself and allow your unique personality to shine through in your speech.

2.5. Reflecting on Your Performance

After your speech, collect constructive feedback and reflect on your performance. Consider your body language, voice modulation, content delivery, and how well you engaged your audience. This planned reflection will help you identify areas of strength and improvement for future speeches.

2.6. Overcoming Public Speaking Anxiety

Fear of public speaking, or glossophobia, is a common challenge, even for veteran speakers. Here are some strategies to overcome speaker anxiety:

1. Practice.

2. Visualization: Picture yourself delivering a successful speech.

3. Deep Breathing.

4. Positive Affirmations.

5. Attempt smaller groups before large audiences.

Public speaking is a skill that can be developed with time, patience, and practice. By understanding the basics, you can embark on your journey toward becoming a dynamic and effective speaker. Embrace the challenge and let your voice be heard.

Chapter 3. Assertiveness 101: Understanding the Concept

Assertiveness is a concept that goes far beyond just saying what you think or feel. It's an effective communication style that involves a balance of expressing your thoughts and beliefs while respecting the rights and belief of others.

Being assertive is about standing up for your rights in a way that doesn't infringe on the rights of others. It requires confidence, self-belief, and the ability to articulate your thoughts effectively.

3.1. The Nature of Assertiveness

Assertiveness is founded on a few key principles - respect, clarity, lack of anxiety, and positive self-image. It is the middle ground between passivity and aggression. Understanding and mastering assertiveness means navigating away from these extremes to harness the positive aspects of both.

When you are assertive, you actively listen to others' views and opinions, showing respect for their thoughts. However, you also ensure that your viewpoint is heard and considered, bringing clarity to the conversation. This requires a level of calm, no presence of unnecessary anxiety, and a positive self-image, free from self-doubt and fear of rejection.

Grasping the in-depth nature of assertiveness can require practice and perseverance. Rest assured, with time and effort, you can cultivate assertiveness as a habit aligned with your normal communication style.

3.2. Assertiveness vs Aggression

Some people confuse assertiveness and aggression, but they are miles apart. Aggression involves violating other people's rights to put your viewpoint forward. Aggressive communicators can come off as dismissive, intimidating and unnecessarily confrontational. To put it bluntly, aggression is disrespect and dominance, while assertiveness is about expressing one's views with respect and balance.

Being assertive means you stand firm, articulate your position without fear, yet ensure your communication doesn't lead to conflict or hurt other people's sentiments. An assertive speaker has the remarkable ability to disagree without being disagreeable.

3.3. Importance of Assertiveness in Public Speaking

Establishing a presence and commanding attention in public speaking requires a blend of strong content and an assertive presentation manner. An assertive speaker is confident, clear, and concise. They respect their audience's time and attention, which in turn commands respect and attention from the audience.

Good public speakers understand the difference between assertiveness and aggressiveness, embracing the former for a balanced, even-handed communication style that engages and captures the audience.

Assertive speakers make the audience feel listened to and valued. They achieve this by delivering clear messages, engaging with the audience, and respecting audience feedback, even when it's negative or challenging. This approachable style fosters a positive atmosphere, which ultimately leads to a better connection with the audience and a more successful performance.

3.4. Achieving an Assertive Communication Style

Here are some practical steps to help you develop assertive communication:

1. Be Clear and Precise: Keep your sentences short and focused. Use simple language, and be precise in what you want to communicate.

2. Learn to Say No: Learning to say no is a powerful tool in your assertiveness toolkit. Don't agree just to avoid a conflict.

3. Master Non-Verbal Communication: Your body language, eye contact, and tone of voice play as much a role in communication as do your words.

4. Practice Active Listening: Demonstrating that you're engaged and interested can reassure the speaker they're being heard.

5. Deal with Criticism Objectively: Detach yourself from your ideas when they're being criticized. Objectively consider the feedback, and respond, instead of react.

As with any new skill, becoming assertive takes practice. Observe assertive communication styles of public figures, practice your speeches in front of colleagues and friends, actively seek out constructive criticism, and iteratively work on it.

Remember, assertiveness is a continuous journey, not a destination. Every conversation, every speech, and every presentation is an opportunity to improve and showcase your assertive communication ability.

3.5. In a Nutshell

Assertiveness is an essential tool for effective public speaking. It plays a pivotal role in how your message is received. Developing assertiveness requires understanding its nature, mastering the art of active listening, clear communication, handling criticism constructively, and constant practice.

By mastering assertiveness, you unlock the ability to convey your messages clearly, effectively, and respectfully, thereby commanding the attention and respect of your audience. With this tool in hand, the formidable stage becomes nothing more than an opportunity to connect, communicate and inspire.

Chapter 4. Building Confidence: Step into Your Power

Meeting your audience or addressing a crowd can be an intimidating prospect. However, having confidence in yourself is a prerequisite for effective public speaking. This confidence is not an overnight luxury but is cultivated and nurtured over time. Here, we unwrap the journey of building confidence, so you can step into your power and command the stage.

4.1. Understanding Confidence

Confidence is a belief in oneself, the conviction that one has the ability to meet life's challenges and to succeed, and the willingness to act accordingly. Being confident requires a realistic sense of one's capabilities and feeling secure in that knowledge.

When you engage in public speaking, confidence acts as a pillar of strength, reinforcing your message and influencing your audience. It helps you maintain eye contact, use bold, clear, and expressive language, and manage pre-speech anxiety.

However, confidence isn't a trait that people either possess or do not. Instead, it can be honed and developed overtime through understanding, practice, and resilience.

4.2. Importance of Self-Talk

Our inner dialogue significantly impacts how we perceive ourselves, which subsequently molds our confidence. Negative self-talk can cripple self-esteem, while positive self-talk can buoy it. One powerful tool to enhance positive self-talk is affirmations - positive statements that can help you to challenge and overcome self-sabotaging and negative thoughts.

Start by identifying negative thoughts and reframing these into affirmative, constructive statements. Repeat these affirmations daily, and you will notice a gradual shift in your mindset and self-perception, laying the groundwork for strong self-confidence.

4.3. Emphasize Body Language

Body language is a non-verbal form of communication that, when applied effectively can exude confidence. From maintaining an upright posture to implementing hand gestures and making eye contact, each element of your body language can effectively enhance your appearance of confidence.

Again, like the skill of public speaking, positive body language is something you can develop with consistent practice. Attend workshops or watch videos of accomplished public speakers. Observe their body language and apply those principals in your own practice sessions.

4.4. Dress for Confidence

How we present ourselves visually significantly impacts the perception of our persona, and consequently, our confidence. Ensure to dress professionally and appropriately for every public speaking opportunity. By doing so, you are not only respecting your audience but also promoting your self-confidence.

Dressing professionally doesn't necessarily mean wearing an expensive suit or dress. Instead, rely on your comfort while adhering to the dress codes defined for the occasion.

4.5. Master Your Material

A crucial aspect of establishing confidence resides in your command over the material. Know your message inside and out, to reduce the anxiety of forgetting lines or being caught unprepared.

Invest considerable time in understanding your topic, undertake thorough research, and rehearse your presentation diligently. Applying mnemonics and using presentation tools can assist in recalling facts, figures, or specific points that you want to highlight.

4.6. Seek Constructive Feedback

Feedback can intimidate many of us, but it's one of the most powerful tools for growth and improvement. Constructive feedback and criticism can shed light on areas that need work, fostering a deeper understanding of your strengths and weaknesses.

Regularly seek feedback from mentors, colleagues, or your public speaking coach. Respond to feedback with gratitude and openness, utilizing insights to enhance your future performances.

4.7. Embrace Failure

Building confidence is not about never failing but learning from failures. Embrace failure as a stepping stone on your road to success. Understand that even the most influential public speaking greats have had their share of failures.

Each time you make a mistake, see it as an opportunity for growth and development. Instead of dwelling on the disappointment or embarrassment, focus on the lesson each mishap provides.

4.8. Nurture Your Well-Being

Physical and mental well-being play an essential role in creating and maintaining confidence. Regular exercise, a balanced diet, and adequate sleep can have a direct impact on your self-esteem.

Moreover, nurturing your mental health through practices like meditation, breathing exercises, or journaling can also significantly boost your confidence. By taking care of yourself, you are affirming your worth, thus building the scaffolding for robust self-confidence.

Remember, confidence-building is a continual process. Embrace the journey, celebrate the small achievements along the way, and step into your power. The stage is waiting for you, all you have to do is radiate your newfound confidence and own it. With your bolstered confidence, you will be able to captivate your audience and leave an unforgettable impression.

Chapter 5. The Power of Voice: Techniques for Effective Delivery

Effective communication is more than just correctly stringed words. Our voice – its volume, pace, inflection and tone – enormously impacts the efficiency of our delivery. Transforming how you use your voice can drastically improve your audience's reaction to your public speech or presentation, shaping their understanding, engagement, and reception. This section holds the key to the castle, offering you unique techniques to magnify your speech delivery with the power of voice.

5.1. Understanding Your Voice

Voice is an instrument, and like any good musician, understanding its capabilities and limitations is crucial. It's sometimes astonishing just how much of an impact your voice can have on an audience. The richness, the timbre, the rhythm - everything mixes to create a symphony that can help you connect with your listeners on a deeper level.

Let's dissect the intricacies of our voice:

1. Vocabulary: The words you choose can trigger different emotional responses in your audience. A powerful vocabulary allows for clearer communication, greater precision, and increased listener engagement.

2. Volume: Using the right volume helps your audience to hang on every word you say. If too low, they may tune you out; too high, and the speech becomes overwhelming or aggressive.

3. Pace: The speed at which you speak can affect the listener's

comprehension. A slow pace can suggest wisdom or importance, while a fast pace can reflect excitement or urgency.

4. Pitch: Variations in pitch - the highs and lows of your voice - can keep the audience interested, while a monotonous voice can be off-putting.

5. Pause: Pauses can be very powerful when used effectively, providing a structure to your speech, emphasizing important points, and even creating suspense.

In order to harness these key voicing attributes appropriately, you need to practice and grow comfortable using them.

5.2. Fine-Tuning Your Voice

To enhance your speech delivery, start by refining your voice with the following techniques:

1. Voice Exercises: Just like how you would warm up before an exercise, doing voice exercises before a speech will tune your vocal cords and infuse dynamism in your presentation. These exercises can range from yawning to humming or even some articulation drills.

2. Hydration: A simple but highly effective trick is to keep hydrated. It helps keep your throat moist, which helps in voice modulation and prevents your voice from cracking up.

3. Posture: A good posture is not only visually impressive but also impacts your voice. It allows your lungs to fill up properly and voice to project better.

Always remember to regularly take care of your voice. Maintain good vocal health by avoiding habits that could strain your voice such as smoking or excessive consumption of caffeine or alcohol.

5.3. Voice Modulation Techniques

Voice modulation plays a significant role in delivering an engaging and effective speech. Here are some techniques to master the art:

1. Inflection: Altering the tone of your voice can add color and emotion to your speech. You can use inflection to emphasize key points or to convey surprise, delight, discontent, or a myriad of other emotions.

2. Volume Control: Adjusting the volume can significantly enhance the impact of your delivery. It commands attention. But remember, louder is not always better.

3. Tempo Variation: Varying the speed at which you deliver your speech can create tension, excitement, or calm. Use it judiciously to create the required effect.

4. Powerful Pausing: Using pauses can create dramatic or thoughtful silences, giving your audience time to absorb what you've just said before you move to the next point.

5. Honoring Punctuation: Punctuation isn't just for the written word. Respecting pauses at commas, full stops, or other punctuation can make your speech easier to understand and follow.

5.4. Practice Makes Perfect

The key to sharpening your voice skills is rehearsing and getting constructive feedback. Record your speeches to understand where you need to improve and practice in front of a friendly audience to gain confidence. Remember, becoming a powerful public speaker doesn't happen overnight, and it requires consistent effort, practice, and a continuous learning mindset.

Embrace your voice and its potential for impact - it is one of your most powerful tools in mastering the art of public speaking.

Mastering the use of your voice won't necessarily make you a perfect speaker, but it will undeniably get you closer to becoming one. It's a journey that begins with knowledge, continues with practice, and is completed through constant refinement. Be patient with yourself, stay diligent, and watch as your voice steadily transforms from being 'just another voice in the room' to one that captures and commands attention.

Chapter 6. Mastering Body Language: Silent yet Powerful Communication

Body language, being primarily a visual form of communication, has an immense impact on public speaking scenarios. Unlike verbal speech, it is not solely restricted to or dependent on words. Instead, it involves various elements such as facial expressions, hand gestures, postures, and movements that can express a range of emotions, attitudes, or reactions more accurately and comprehensively than just words could ever do. Therefore, as a public speaker, it is crucial to develop and master such non-verbal communication skills.

6.1. Understanding the Basics of Body Language.

Our body speaks volumes even when we remain silent. Different parts of our body like the face, eyes, hands, legs, torso, all convey distinct messages. A clenched jaw or a frown may signify stress or anger. On the other hand, an open posture and direct eye contact can communicate confidence and sincerity. Understanding this language of the body and knowing how to use it effectively can greatly enhance your presence on the stage and your ability to influence your audience.

When focusing on our body movements and expressions, it's crucial to think about the following components:

Eye Contact: Maintaining steady eye contact with your audience establishes a sense of connection and trust. It's a way to show your audience that you're engaged, confident, and honest about your message.

Facial Expressions: Your facial expressions convey your emotions. When your face is expressive, you appear more approachable and relatable. However, avoid exaggerated expressions as they may compromise your authenticity.

Gestures: Hand gestures can emphasize certain points, make your statements more vivid, and generally maintain the audience's interest. Too many wild gestures, though, can distract from your message, so it's important to find a balance.

Posture: The way you hold yourself can send significant messages about your confidence and authority. Standing tall shows that you're composed and credible, while slouching can suggest insecurity and uncertainty.

6.2. Reading Your Audience's Body Language.

Just as your body language sends messages to your audience, their body language sends messages back to you. You can gauge audience engagement and the effectiveness of your presentation by examining their facial expressions, posture, and gestures. For instance, closed postures like crossed arms might suggest resistance or disengagement while nodding or leaning forward might signify agreement and interest.

6.3. Practicing and Modifying Your Body Language.

Embarking on the journey towards mastering body language requires consistent practicing and conscious efforts. Hence, giving yourself ample opportunities to practice in front of a mirror or videotaping your speeches can serve exceptionally well. You can observe, assess, and modify your body language, making it more articulate and aligned with your verbal speech.

6.4. How to Use Body Language Effectively.

Body language doesn't just involve the speaker's actions; it's also about timing, intensity, and appropriateness. Here are ways to use it effectively:

Consistency: Strive for consistency between your words and your body language. If there's a contradiction between the two, your audience might feel confused, which might undermine your credibility.

Less is More: Overusing gestures can distract your audience. Stick to necessary and natural movements that will enhance rather than detract from your message.

Judicious Use of Space: Depending on the size of your stage or platform, utilize the space wisely. Moving around can show comfort and confidence, but if it's not managed well, it may come off as nervousness or confusion.

6.5. Enhancing Confidence: The Power Pose.

The Power Pose, popularized by social psychologist Amy Cuddy, is a two-minute strategy that involves adopting high power posture - standing tall, hands on the hips, shoulders squared. This pose can stimulate a hormonal response, reducing stress and boosting confidence.

In conclusion, the mastery of body language is a step towards becoming a dynamic communicator. As daunting as it may seem initially, with continuous practice and a keen understanding of the basics, you can harness the full power of non-verbal communication, using it to engage, inspire, and influence your audience in ways that words alone can't achieve.

Chapter 7. Crafting Impactful Speeches: The Art of Effective Preparation

Public speaking is often seen as a difficult skill to master, but a large part of your success hinges on effective preparation. To craft an impactful speech, preparation has to be meticulous, thorough, and aimed at making your content as engaging as possible. It involves understanding your audience, creating a compelling message, structuring your speech for maximum impact, rehearsing out loud, and preparing for the unexpected. Let's dig deep into these aspects to give you an effective guide to preparing impactful speeches.

7.1. Know Your Audience

The first and most vital part of speech preparation is understanding your audience. A speech, after all, is a form of conversation, albeit one-sided. To make it engaging and meaningful, your content must be relatable and significant to your audience. Here is a step by step guide:

1. Identify the demographics: Start by understanding the basic demographic information of your audience - age, gender, location, educational background, etc. It helps design content that resonates with them.

2. Understand their interests: What does your audience care about? What are their hopes, fears, and motivations? Unearth these crucial pieces of information to make your content more relatable.

3. Perceive their expectations: Gauge precisely what your audience expects from your speech. Are they seeking information, inspiration, or entertainment? Tailor your content to match these

expectations to captivate their attention effectively.

4. Analyze the cultural context: Everyone is shaped by the culture they live in. Be sure to consider cultural backgrounds as you craft your speech to ensure your content is sensitive and be received positively.

7.2. Structuring Your Speech

Structuring your speech carefully allows your audience to follow your message more easily. The golden rule is to follow a three-part structure—introduction, body, and conclusion. However, within these three parts, there are certain elements that should be considered to enhance the impact and clarity of your message.

7.3. Introduction

Hook your audience early with an intriguing introduction. Your first few sentences should capture your audience's attention and make them want to listen to your speech. Here are some techniques:

1. Start with a powerful quote or statistic.

2. Share a compelling story or anecdote.

3. Pose a thought-provoking question.

4. Use humor judiciously to lighten the mood.

State your speech objective clearly, so your audience knows what to expect. Declaring your content from the start allows your audience to mentally prepare for your speech, making it easier for them to follow your points.

7.4. Body

This is the part where you deliver the bulk of your content. Break your body into several key points or ideas, each substantiated with facts, evidence, and examples. Remember to:

1. Stay focused and avoid deviating from your main points.

2. Use transitions to guide your audience through your logic and ensure flow between points.

3. Use visual aids where possible to enhance understanding.

4. Keep language and concepts understandable and accessible.

7.5. Conclusion

Your conclusion should create a powerful and lasting impression. Restate your main points and reinforce your speech objective. You may strategize by:

1. Ending with a call to action, prompting your audience to respond in some way.

2. Summarizing your key points.

3. Closing with a provocative question or statement to make your speech memorable.

7.6. Practicing Out Loud

Even the most well-prepared speech can fall flat without proper rehearsal. Practicing out loud does not mean merely going over your content; it is about experiencing your speech as your audience would.

1. Go through your speech from start to finish without breaks.

2. Pay attention to your voice modulation, pace, and emphasis.

3. Practice your speech in the context you'll deliver it—standing if you'll be standing.

4. Record your practice and listen critically.

7.7. **Prepare for the Unexpected**

Sometimes things don't go as planned. Being prepared for the unexpected nuances ensures you stay poised and collected.

1. Prepare for equipment failure: Always have a backup plan, just in case your presentation tools fail.

2. Know your material: Even if your slide presentation fails, know your material thoroughly so that you can continue without it.

3. Handle questions wisely: Respond thoughtfully and honestly. If you aren't sure, it is okay to clarify and respond later.

Keep in mind that not everything depends on the day of the speech. The lion's share of your success lies in your preparation phase. Properly understanding your audience, structuring your speech, practicing out loud, and preparing for the unexpected can set you up for success and allow you to deliver a truly impactful speech.

Chapter 8. Using Assertiveness Techniques in Real-Time Scenarios

Assertiveness is a crucial trait to manifest effectively in public speaking. Not only does it lend credibility to your expressions, but it also substantiates your presence, radiating a distinct level of respect and authority. To harness assertiveness techniques in real-time scenarios, let's delve into these steps systematically.

8.1. Understanding Assertiveness

Assertiveness refers to a communicative balance retaining the respect for oneself as well as others. An assertive speaker strikes a balance between passivity and aggression, gently enforcing their viewpoint without trampling over others. It's a practice of open, direct, and honest communication that ultimately sparks fruitful discussions.

Understanding assertiveness is the first step towards its real-time application. Assertiveness allows you to express yourself without succumbing to fear or anxiety, and serves as a pillar for constructive dialogue. Accepting this as a significant aspect of your presentation or speaking task, paves the way to master it further.

8.2. The Pillars of Assertiveness

There are four major components to becoming assertive in your public speaking endeavors – clarity, empathy, respect, and control.

- *Clarity.* It's important to clearly express your thoughts, feelings, and needs. Unclear messages can sow confusion and might not have the desired impact. So, before you speak, ensure you have the clarity of thoughts and expressions.

- *Empathy.* Demonstrating empathy generates a mutual respect between the speaker and the listener. When addressing a crowd, ensure that you understand and consider the feelings of your listeners.

- *Respect.* Show respect for others and honor their opinions – even if they differ from your own. This helps in creating a mutual understanding that fosters clean, rewarding communication.

- *Control.* Your emotional control can influence how your message is received. While passion is good, excessive emotion may cloud the real message. Maintain your composure and stay in control of your emotions when you speak.

8.3. Assertiveness Techniques for Public Speaking

Presentation techniques can effectively enhance your assertive communication skills. It's then not about changing who you are, but how you communicate your ideas.

- *The 'Broken Record' Technique.* Repeat your main point or request over and over again, in a calm manner, regardless of the responses you receive. This strategy reinforces your message and keeps you focused on your agenda.

- *The 'Fogging' Technique.* This technique helps to stay assertive in controversial or heated scenarios. Accept criticism — whether constructive or otherwise — without becoming defensive. You can agree with any truth present in the criticism without agreeing to the negativity attached to it, hence maintaining control of the conversation.

- *The 'Free Information' Technique.* Give more information than asked for. It helps keep the conversation going and places you as a knowledge source while asserting your command over the topic discussed.

- *The 'Negative Inquiry' Technique.* Encourage your critics or detractors to expand on their criticism. This approach not only gives you an opportunity to understand their viewpoint better, but also helps maintain an open, non-defensive demeanor.

8.4. Assertiveness Skills in Real-Life Scenarios

Turning theory into practice may seem challenging initially, but with practice and persistence, the transition becomes smooth.

- *Networking Events.* At such gatherings, leverage the 'Free Information' technique to keep conversations flowing and to establish yourself as a thought leader. Repeatedly using your main points ('Broken Record' technique) will also help to reinforce your professional identity.

- *Public Presentations.* For public speeches, adopt the 'Fogging' technique to respond to criticism effectively, without derailing your narrative. Clarity, control, respect, and empathy can help build a rapport with your listeners and make you an effective presenter.

- *Work Meetings.* Use the 'Negative Inquiry' and 'Broken Record' techniques when defending your proposals during work meetings. They offer an avenue to understand objections better, while attaining your end goal. Assertiveness here includes conveying your points concisely and respectfully, and maintaining your composure.

Assertiveness does not come naturally to everyone. But, with a comprehensive understanding, the right techniques, and applied practice, anyone can master the art of assertive communication. As with any skill, enriching your assertiveness takes time. Start small, practice regularly, and gradually, you would notice yourself growing into a more confident, composed, and charismatic speaker.

Chapter 9. Managing Anxiety and Nerves: Stay Calm & Confident

One cannot flick a switch and suddenly become a masterful public speaker, immune to anxiety and nerves. Alas, as humans, these fears come naturally to us, especially when faced with the prospect of public speaking. Yet, it is not an insurmountable challenge. Regulating anxiety and nerves is possible, it simply requires understanding, practice, and technique.

9.1. Understand Your Anxiety

It's normal to feel anxious before and during a public speaking event. After all, our ancestors needed to react swiftly to real, immediate threats like predators - it's that age-old fight, flight, or freeze response kicking in. Only now, your sabertooth tiger is a crowd of spectators.

Anxiety manifests itself differently in each individual. Recognizing your own unique anxiety indicators is the initial step towards managing them. You might get sweaty palms, a racing heart, lightheadedness, or maybe you begin fidgeting uncontrollably. Take note of these reactions. Understand your body's symptoms of anxiety so that you can identify when your nerves start kicking in.

9.2. Reframing Anxiety as Excitement

Shift the narrative of your anxiety. Let's make one thing clear: anxiety and excitement are two sides of the same coin. They are both aroused emotions, but one is negative, while the other is positive. You can trick your brain into transforming that anxiety into excitement. This doesn't mean ignoring your anxiety, but instead approaching it with a different perspective.

Instead of telling yourself, "I'm anxious about this speech," shift your perspective and rephrase it to, "I'm excited to share my ideas with the audience." Changing this narrative can lead to a shift in how you physically feel, helping to cultivate a sense of excitement rather than dread.

9.3. Preparing and Practicing Your Speech

A key strategy to combat anxiety is by being prepared. Familiarize yourself with your speech content. The more comfortable you are with what you're speaking about, the easier it becomes to communicate confidently.

Remember, practicing isn't simply about repetition; it's about improving and refining each time you run through your speech. Effective practicing includes speaking aloud, employing gestures, and using visual aids as you would in the actual presentation. Record yourself if possible, and review areas where you stumble or seem uncertain.

Finally, rehearse in front of a small audience - friends, family, or colleagues. They can give constructive feedback which might prove beneficial.

9.4. Power Poses and Physical Relaxation Techniques

Your body language communicates volumes without you uttering a single word. Power posing, or assuming postures of confidence, has been shown to reduce stress and increase feelings of empowerment. Stand tall, take up space, and open your arms. This can promote hormonal changes in your body, heightening your confidence and reducing nervousness.

Along with power poses, physical relaxation techniques can also be incredibly beneficial. These techniques stretch across a spectrum, from deep breathing exercises to progressive muscle relaxation, where you tense and relax different muscle groups in your body. Experiment with these techniques and channel the ones that work best for you.

9.5. Visualize Your Success

Visualization is a powerful tool that helps solidify a successful performance in your mind. Imagine yourself standing in front of your audience, delivering your speech with authority, confidence, and flair. Picture your listeners, engaged and engrossed. Visualizing these positive responses can be a big mental boost.

9.6. Leverage Nervous Energy

Lastly, use your jitters to your advantage! Convert the nervous energy into a dynamic, passionate presentation. A certain amount of adrenaline can sharpen your performance, making you more alive and engaging. Instead of fighting your anxiety, find a way to channel it into your presentation. Breathe, harness it, and let it lend intensity to your message.

All these techniques and strategies might not eliminate your anxiety completely – but they will help manage it to a large extent. Consistency is the key. Keep at it and eventually, your confidence will outweigh your anxiety, making you a more dynamic, assertive, and engaging public speaker.

Chapter 10. Interacting with the Audience: Learn to Engage Effectively

Regardless of what you're presenting, the goal is most likely to engage your audience. A truly successful presentation is one in which the audience, not just the speaker, actively participates. Here are some key concepts and concrete steps you can take to make your interactions with the audience effective, dynamic and meaningful.

10.1. Understand Your Audience

The first step toward effective audience engagement is understanding your audience. Know their needs, their interests, their familiarity with your topic, and the cultural or professional context in which they're operating.

Before your presentation, research your audience's demographics, knowledge levels, and preferences. Use surveys or pre-event meetings to gather information. Even informal conversations can provide valuable insights. You can also revisit past presentations, if applicable, to discern their response patterns.

10.2. Understand Your Content

Your mastery of the subject matter will help you anticipate audience reactions and questions. You must know your material inside and out in order to present it effectively. As well as clarifying your main points, consider potential points of confusion or controversy and prepare responses in advance. Your preparedness will boost your confidence and, in turn, your credibility with the audience.

10.3. Establish a Connection

Audience engagement is inherently about connection. Use storytelling techniques to make personal links with your listeners. Stories can illuminate complex points and are far more memorable than abstract concepts alone.

Try sharing relevant experiences, making them as relatable as possible. Use humor when appropriate – laughter can break down barriers and create a shared experience. Be authentic. Your audience will appreciate your honesty and be more willing to engage.

10.4. Encourage Interaction

Instead of delivering a monologue, aim to start a dialogue. Encourage questions and comments by creating spaces for interaction throughout your presentation. Pause strategically to invite audience feedback or queries.

You can also use interactive activities to involve the audience. This may range from simple question-and-answer sessions, to hands-on demonstrations, quizzes, or group discussions. Such activities can break the rhythm of a one-sided presentation and keep the audience significantly more engaged.

10.5. Look and Listen

Visual and auditory clues can tell you a lot about your audience's engagement level. Are they distracted or attentive? Are they understanding your points or do they seem confused? Identify signs of disengagement, such as fidgeting or side conversations, and change your tactics accordingly.

Listening to your audience is equally important. When they ask questions or make comments, respond thoughtfully and carefully.

Make sure your responses align with their concerns or ideas. It tells your audience that you value their input and enhances your rapport.

10.6. Use Visual Aids

Visual aids can be powerful tools to enhance your message, provided they are used judiciously. Slides, diagrams, charts, infographics can add interest, clarify complex points and improve your audience's recall.

Remember - visual aids should support, not overpower your message. Keep them simple and relevant, and control their use so they enhance and do not detract from your main points.

10.7. Overcome Challenges

You may encounter disruptions, difficult questions, or disinterested audience members. In such cases, stay calm and composed. If faced with a difficult question, take your time and provide the best answer possible, even if that means admitting your lack of knowledge and promising to find the answer later.

For disruptions or challenging behaviour, try to address the situation without losing your cool or being overly confrontational. It's important to maintain a professional demeanor and to keep the focus on your message.

In summary, effective audience engagement during public speaking largely relies on understanding your audience, mastering your content, encouraging interaction, and using body language and visual aids effectively. By implementing these guides, you are bound to transform your presentations and speeches, drawing audiences in, holding their attention, and leaving them with valuable insights.

Chapter 11. Continuous Improvement: Tools and Techniques for Ongoing Growth

"Continuous improvement" is a term often thrown around in the corporate world. But what exactly does it mean when it comes to equipping ourselves with the mastery of public speaking? At its core, continuous improvement refers to the practice of striving for personal and professional excellence in small increments, rather than attempting large disruptive changes.

This chapter sheds light on the vital tools and techniques that will help you remain on a trajectory of continuous growth in your public speaking skills. With the ideas we explore here, you'll be equipped to learn from your experiences and make the necessary adjustments to hone your communication abilities. It's not a quick fix, nor a one-size-fits-all solution, but it's a commitment to enhancement that makes all the difference in the long haul.

11.1. Honing a Growth Mindset

A growth mindset is paramount for continuous improvement in any field, including public speaking. When you have a growth mindset, you believe that skills can be developed through efforts, persistence, and hard work. Thus, you are more open to taking on challenges and view failures or obstacles as opportunities to learn and grow.

To foster a growth mindset, start by acknowledging that success isn't immediate but occurs over time. Also, open your mind to receive constructive feedback and use it for improvement rather than taking it personally or defensively. Lastly, make it a habit to reflect on your speeches or presentations and identify the areas where you did well and areas needing improvement.

11.2. Embracing the Power of Reflection

Reflection, in simple terms, means stepping back to ponder about past speaking experiences. What did you do well? What could be improved? Did you reach your communication goals? By asking these questions, we begin to shine a light on areas for our improvement.

As a public speaker, it should become second nature for you to evaluate each speech on your own. A simple way to do this is through reflective journaling. Write down key points from your presentation: what you did well, what went wrong, what felt awkward or fluid, audience reactions, etc. After some cooling-off time—at least a day—reread your notes and analyze those inputs to learn and improve.

11.3. Implementing Feedback Loops

A feedback loop refers to the process of using the results of an action for the following steps. The idea is to continuously adjust and improve based on the received criticism. Making the most out of feedback, whether from your audience, coach or peer group, can yield massive improvements in public speaking.

While it might be hard to listen to criticism, especially when you've invested a lot of effort into a speech or presentation, it's one of the keys to growth as a speaker. Take note of every piece of feedback and, without taking it personally, use this information to refine your skills. From eye contact and body language to voice modulation and visual aids—feedback can help you identify areas of improvement.

11.4. The Art of Incremental Changes

Often, the most daunting tasks can become manageable when we break them down into small, achievable steps. The same philosophy applies to public speaking. By applying incremental changes in your speeches, you can gradually improve your skills while diluting the fear of public speaking.

For instance, in your first few attempts, focus on just being audible enough. With a few more tries, work on your body language. Next, try bettering your content. Divide each broad aspect of public speaking into a smaller subset and work on them one by one. This will not only provide you with achievable targets but also boost your confidence as you see visible improvements.

11.5. Constant Practice and Exposure

There's an old saying that practice makes perfect. This, of course, is a bit of an exaggeration because nobody is truly perfect. However, regular practice can most certainly push you closer to excellence.

Consider joining a public speaking club or association, which will provide you with frequent opportunities to speak in front of a supportive group. By continuously putting yourself out there, you get an opportunity to work on the different aspects of public speaking and receive a wide variety of feedback.

11.6. Learning from Others

Observe others who are accomplished at the skill you want to foster. By watching experienced speakers, you can pick up on their techniques and styles, learning what works and importantly, what might work for you. Ted Talks, webinars, and professional speaking engagements are excellent platforms for learning from others. Absorb their storytelling skills, their power of expression, gauging audience reactions—they are live repositories of lessons to learn.

11.7. Conclusion

The path to mastering public speaking is a journey of constant evaluation, willingness to accept feedback, regular practice, and reflection. It's about honing your style, refining your delivery, and remaining open to change. It's a journey without a destination, for there is always room for improvement. You will deliver speeches that deeply resonate with the audience, and some, that don't quite hit the mark. But through them all, ensure there is incremental growth and continued learning. With this commitment to continuous improvement, you'll be well on your way to mastering public speaking.